WHY DON'T WORMS HAVE LEGS?

By Rebecca Storm

CONTENTS

First published in 2026 by
Hungry Tomato Ltd
F15, Old Bakery Studios, Blewetts Wharf, Malpas Road,
Truro, Cornwall, TR1 1QH, UK.

Thanks to our editor, Julie Tofflemire.

A CIP catalog record for this book is available from the British Library.

ISBN 9781835694381
Manufactured in the USA

Discover more at
www.hungrytomato.com

All words in **BOLD** can be found in the glossary.

WHICH ANIMALS HAVE YOU SEEN OUT IN NATURE?

Nature is filled with lots of little creatures.
You have probably seen lots of them in your backyard or a park.

Some creatures live in water. Some live among the plants. Some build nests, and others live underground.

But do you know what these creatures do in their wildlife homes? What do they eat? And how do they care for their young?

WHICH INSECT MAKES HONEY?

Insects called bees make honey.

Worker bees collect **nectar** from flowers.

They turn it into honey inside their bodies.

When a bee finds flowers with plenty of nectar, it goes back to the hive and does a kind of dance.

The dance shows the other bees which direction to go to find flowers. They can all collect plenty of nectar.

Beehives don't always look the same!

Human-made beehive

Wild beehive

In the hive, the bees make waxy combs that they fill with the honey.

WHAT ARE LARVAE?

In the combs are the young bees. They are called **larvae**. Just one is called a **larva**.

Worker bees feed the larvae with honey.

Beekeepers collect the combs and remove the honey from them. They leave some for the bees.

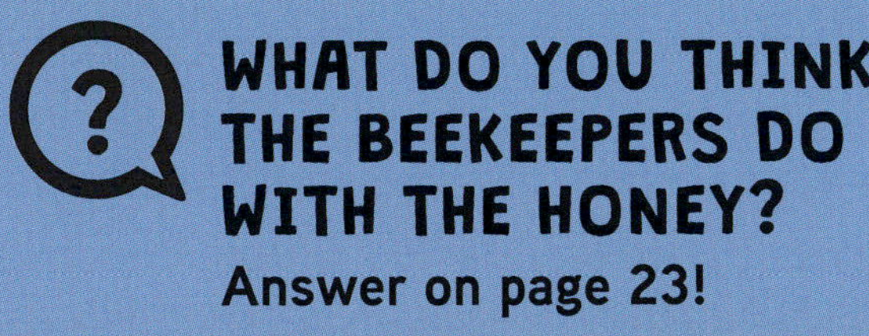

HOW DOES A SPIDER MAKE ITS WEB?

A spider makes its web from threads of **silk** it gets from inside its own body.

The silk is thin, but it is very strong!

HOW DOES A SPIDER BUILD A WEB?

The spider starts by stretching just one thread of silk between two leaves or twigs. Then it fixes another thread to another leaf or twig.

It makes a shape like the **spokes** of a wheel. Then it fills in the spaces between the spokes.

Different kinds of spiders make different kinds of webs. Funnel webs and orb webs are just two examples.

CATCHING FOOD

The web traps insects that the spider can eat.

Spiders are very useful. Their webs often trap **pests** such as flies.

WHICH IS STRONGER — STEEL WIRE OR A SPIDER'S SILK?
Answer on page 23!

WHAT DOES A CATERPILLAR TURN INTO?

When it has grown to its full size, a caterpillar turns into a butterfly!

Caterpillars **hatch** from tiny eggs.

Each caterpillar eats and eats and grows and grows.

When the caterpillar gets too big for its skin, the skin falls off! There is a new one underneath.

The caterpillar goes on growing and gets another new skin. This happens several times.

After a while, the caterpillar makes a shell for itself. Now it is called a **pupa**.

Something amazing happens inside the pupa.

Unlike caterpillars, butterflies do not eat leaves – but they do lay eggs on them.

WHAT DO YOU THINK HAPPENS TO BUTTERFLY EGGS?
Answer on page 23!

WHAT DO ANTS DO ALL DAY?

Ants work hard all day looking after their nest.

Some ants are "soldiers". They defend the nest.

The **queen ant** lays eggs in the nest. Most ants are "workers". Some look after the eggs. Others find food and protect the nest.

Queen ant

Newly hatched ants

Larvae hatch from the eggs. Workers bring food for the larvae.

The larvae make **cocoons**. Inside the cocoons, they turn into adult ants. Some workers look after the cocoons.

WHAT DO ANTS COLLECT?

Some ants collect **honeydew** from insects called **aphids**.

Ants stroke the aphids to make them release honeydew from their bodies.

WHAT DO YOU THINK THE ANTS USE THE HONEYDEW FOR?

Answer on page 23!

WHY DON'T WORMS HAVE LEGS?

Worms don't have legs because they don't need them to move around under the ground.

A worm's body is made up of parts called **segments**.

There are tiny **bristles**, like hairs, on each segment.

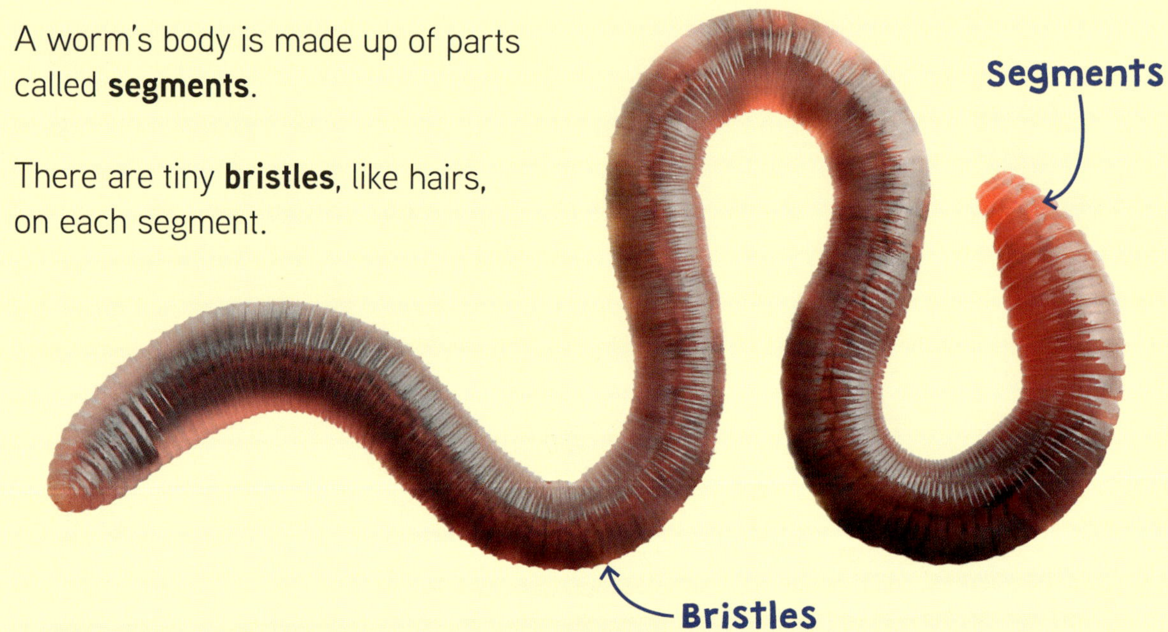

MOVING AROUND

The worm uses the bristles to push itself through the **soil** under the ground.

Worms eat soil, leaves, and animal **droppings**.

Sometimes you can see the **remains** of the worm's meal after it has passed through the worm's body.

The remains are very good for the soil.

DIGGING UNDERGROUND

Worms also make holes or passageways in the soil. The holes make it easier for water to reach the roots of plants.

Worms are very useful in our backyards. Birds like to eat them, too.

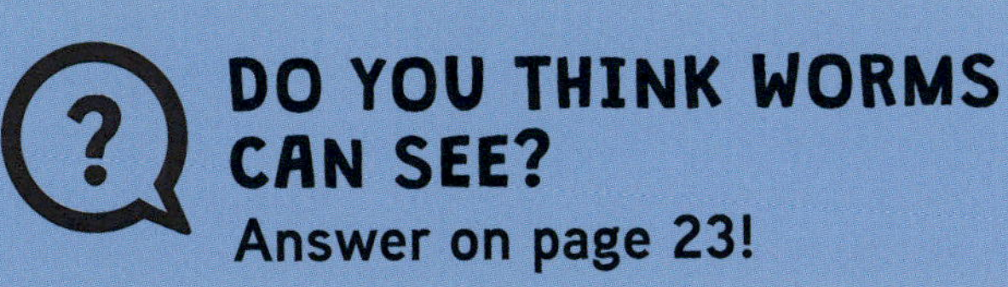

WHAT DOES A BABY FROG LOOK LIKE?

Baby frogs look a bit like fish. They are called tadpoles. The tadpoles start life as tiny dots in a lump of clear jelly. This is **frogspawn**. You may find it in a pond.

Gradually, the dot changes shape and tadpoles hatch out of the frogspawn.

As the tadpoles grow bigger, they change shape.

They grow legs. When they have grown legs and start moving on land, they are called froglets.

Their tails eventually get smaller, then disappear. That's when they are called frogs!

WHICH ANIMALS ARE LIKE FROGS?

Animals with lives like frogs are called **amphibians**. Toads, salamanders, and newts are also amphibians.

Toad

Salamander

Newt

WHY DO GARDENERS LIKE LADYBUGS?

Ladybugs are a kind of **beetle**. Most are red with black spots.

They are helpful in the backyard because they eat aphids.

Aphids suck the juice out of plants, and the plants may die.

HOW MANY APHIDS DO YOU THINK A LADYBUG CAN EAT IN ONE DAY?

Answer on page 23!

LADYBUG LIFE

Ladybugs lay eggs, which their larvae hatch out of.

Ladybug eggs

Ladybug larva

The larvae eat lots of food – they grow bigger and bigger. One day, they will become adult ladybugs.

A GARDENER'S BEST FRIEND

If there are lots of ladybugs in your backyard, they will eat lots of aphids.

The plants will grow well. That's why gardeners like ladybugs.

There are many different kinds of ladybugs.

HOW DO SNAILS MOVE AROUND?

A snail has a foot under its body. It moves around by using this foot to push itself along.

A snail makes slime, called mucus. This helps it slide along.

Snail foot

SHELL SAFETY

The snail can hide inside its shell when it is afraid or when it is very hot outside.

LEAF-MUNCHERS

Gardeners do not like
snails. They eat many
different kinds of plants,
especially young ones.

Snails also eat fruit
and vegetables.

But there are animals that
eat snails.

Snakes, rats, frogs, and toads all eat snails.
So do some kinds of birds and beetles.

HOW BIG DO YOU THINK A SNAIL CAN GROW?

Answer on page 23!

GLOSSARY

Amphibians - Animals that can live in water and on land. Frogs, toads, newts, and salamanders are all different kinds of amphibians.

Aphids - Small insects that suck the juices out of plants. Other names for them are greenflies (if they are green) or blackflies (if they are black).

Beetle - An insect with a hard, shiny covering over its wings.

Bristles - Short, stiff hairs.

Cocoons - Cases made by insects from silk that comes from inside their bodies. Inside its cocoon, the insect changes from a young insect to a grown-up one.

Droppings - Animal waste – poo!

Frogspawn - Frogs' eggs. They look like clear jelly with the young tadpole growing inside. Toads lay the same kind of eggs.

Hatch - To come out of an egg.

Honeydew - A liquid made in the bodies of aphids. Aphids suck the juice from plants and pass it out of their bodies as sweet honeydew.

Insects - Animals that have six legs and a body in three parts. There are thousands of different kinds of insects in the world.

Larva (Larvae) - The young of many kinds of insects are called larvae. One young is called a larva. Caterpillars are the larvae of butterflies.

Nectar - A sweet liquid found inside flowers that lots of insects like to eat.

Pests - Animals that do damage to plants. Many gardeners think of snails as pests because they eat lots of plants.

Pupa - An insect that is changing from being a larva to an adult.

Remains - The parts of something that are left over after being used.

Segments - Parts of something.

Silk - Fine thread produced by spiders from inside their bodies. They use it to make webs. Some other insects also make silk. The silk we use to make fabric for clothes is made by the caterpillars of a kind of moth.

Soil - The top layer of the ground, also called dirt.

Spokes - The parts of a wheel that stick out from the middle to the edge.

Page 7: Beekeepers collect the honey so that we can eat it!

Page 9: A thread of spider's silk is as strong as a piece of steel wire of the same thickness.

Page 11: Tiny caterpillars hatch from butterfly eggs.

Page 13: Worms have no eyes! But they do have parts that can sense light.

Page 15: Ants use honeydew to feed their larvae.

Page 17: Frogs can live in and out of water. Animals that live like this are called amphibians.

Page 18: A ladybug can eat 50 aphids in one day.

Page 21: The average garden snail is smaller than a ping-pong ball. But the giant African land snail's shell can be over 8 inches (20 centimeters) long!

INDEX

Picture credits:
(t=top; b=bottom; m=middle; l=left; r=right):

Adeel Ahmed photos 8b; Aleksandar Dickov 20tr; Aleksandr Rybalko 7t; andregric 10tl; Andrey Pavlov 12mr; Anest 19tl; Anton Kozyrev 19br;BranoMolnar 16b; Chrispo 9ml; DanBekaJourney 20br; Darijus Gurskij 21t; Darkdiamond67 10tr, 11t, 23br; Dirk Daniel Mann 3bg; encierro 19bl; Eric Isselee 17t; greggnormal 16tr; Harry Wedzinga 4-5bg; Henrik Larsson 12br; ifong 8tr; Jakirul777 8ml; Jorge Abel Photography 19tr; Jurga Jot 15ml; Kosobu 21mr; Kurit afshen 17t, 17tmr; Lauren Suryanata 17bm; Litote Photography 20bl;Madhegowdu 9tl; mehmetkrc 18b,18tr; Mezee Ji 6t; Mountains Hunter 12tl; New Africa 7br; nicemyphoto 6br; Nick Greaves 9tr; Nynke van Holten 21br; Ondrej Prosicky 11br; Pavel Krasensky 12bl, 13t; Raseduly 17bl; Sana Rahim 15t; Sari ONeal 10bl; slowmotiongli 7ml; Sugianto88 11m; Szasz-Fabian Jozsef 13ml;Tetiana Tychynska 18br; Valentina Razumova 14t; VaskePro 14bl; W. de Vries 17br; wertinio 6bl; Wirestock Creators 1bg, 15br.

Every effort has been made to trace the copyright holders, and we apologize in advance for any unintentional omissions. We would be pleased to insert the appropriate acknowledgments in any subsequent edition of this publication.